Conversations for a Dreamer of the Dawn

*A collection of poems in English,
from warm days and evenings,
during the seasons and years,
in Britain and Uganda*

Peter Egobu Ebalu

FOUNTAIN PUBLISHERS
Kampala

Fountain Publishers
P.O. Box 488
Kampala
Tel: 256-(41)259163/251112 Fax: 251160
E-mail: fountain@starcom.co.ug
Website: www.fountainpublishers.co.ug

Distributed in Europe, North America and Australia by
African Books Collective Ltd (ABC), Unit 13, Kings
Meadow, Ferry Hinksey Road, Oxford OX2 0DP, United
Kingdom.
Tel: 44(0) 1865-726686, Fax:44(0)1865-793298.
E-mail: abc@africanbookscollective.com
Website: www.africanbookscollective.com

© Peter Egobu Ebalu 2006
First published 2006

All rights reserved. No part of this publication may be reprinted or reproduced or utilised in any form or by any means, electronic, mechanical or other means now known or hereafter invented, including copying and recording, or in any information storage or retrieval system, without permission in writing from the publishers.

ISBN 9970 02 569 4

In Memory

Of Daddy.

*For our late sister Grace
and all who have left us
whom we loved and miss,
live for ever.*

*Most especially I pray each reader will gain
something of worth from reading, memorising,
singing and studying the poetry in this collection
if that is their wish.*

Contents

Bereavement Poems
Why didn't you cry? — 1
I still oppose cynicism — 1
Weak link — 2
Ode to a heroine — 3
A self-assignment brings familiar memories — 4
Aijar na mam edaun — 5
Charity — 6

Nature Poems
Licence to thrill — 7
Memory — 7
Who likes emphasis in the vast view? — 7
The selfish and (therefore) lonely star! — 9
Wrong advice to women! — 9
The Lion King — 9
Life's bends — 9
Ode to autumn — 11
If only — 12
Thou art more than a conqueror, therefore relent — 13
On the way to Uppsala — 14
Make it last forever! — 14

Existentialist Poems
...me — 16
Roll on the future — 16
Open a new chapter — 17
The exile's song — 18
...surrounded by love — 18
Go white horses! — 20
My own man — 21
Proud of this form — 21
The Blues — 22
The Prince of Peace — 22
And on his law they meditate day and night — 23

Rest in Peace	24
The eclectic dream	25
She looked at me	26
When the knight fell	26
Rage against the dying of the light	28
Love always protects	29
A song of the dawn	31

Love Poems

Even after death	35
The end of eternity	35
To the real oasis?	35
The dawning of eternity	35
Solara	36
Beauty strikes!	36
Of a girl I loved to dream	37
A young man dreams of courage	37
Pride	38
Keep your best strength	39
Diamonds love Racquel	40
Ode to someone who used to be special	41
Hope!	42
Journey's song	43
Ode to a foreigner	44
My gentle rhyme	45
Canadian blues of a Ugandan kid	46
Canadian blues by a Ugandan man	47
Ode to an angel	49
To the successful Messiah - what a way to win!	49
Show a little tenderness	50
Dreams may come true	51
A scene we shared beneath the stars in days gone by	52
Lord	53
Now the trek is over	54
Brothers and sisters…	55
Time and tide wait for no-one	56

Bereavement Poems

Why didn't you cry?
This was a world not for your spirit
you lived your life but were not in it,

You were like eagles soaring high
and the bird that could not fly,

It's such a shame you chose to die
when it would have done to hear you cry,

But in your life you touched many
a quiet man who hurt not any,

I'm sorry friend
you changed your mind
and closed that door
left us behind
but when we meet in the starry sky
I really hope you'll tell us why.

* * *

I still oppose cynicism
I wish I could sing with one true voice
and show you some wishes which are now dreams,

I wish I could sing with one true voice
and tell you the evil that I have seen,

Egotistic pride in the destruction
of things that were beautiful once
not in abundance or creation
or the harmonisation of rare inherent beauty,

The things that were beautiful once
that still hold beauty,

The reckless destruction of that which is already weak
rather than the buttressing of that which could be strong
and the strengthening of the weak,

I also wish I could sing with one true voice
and tell you the love that is within.

* * *

Weak link
Carry her far away
from me
for I never want
again to see
her eyes
when pity's all they have
for me,

Take her away,
for you must see
that she no longer
has love for me
and I no longer
want to see
her lightless eyes
gone out to sea,

So, go; take away
your fancy
maybe you'll find
another more than me
who'll keep away

the misery
of being with a man like me.

* * *

Ode to a heroine

I remember how I met her
I remember how I loved her,

I tried to resist but when we talked
I wished to kiss her as we walked,

Because she was so nice
my heart missed a beat thrice,

Such beautiful sensuous grace
and lovely face made me impressed,

O, how I loved her
if only I could tell her,

Maybe one day
not far away
in some secluded place we'll stay
a wonderful true holiday
where dreams can mingle with
the day,

Today instead I'm miles away
from that fantasy of one day
yet I really wish to say
I've missed your love
hope you're okay.

* * *

A self-assignment brings familiar memories
If my loving wasn't good enough
for her
she should have told me so and saved my heart,

I loved her when
I saw her
and then I couldn't ignore her
and I knew I was wrong
and that she'd break my heart
but not even that pain
could keep my love apart,

The pain I feel every day
is because I gave my love away
to my spiritual love
who loved me not within
but loved another of my kin,

What could I do
with my hurt pride
with all the pain I could not hide,

I couldn't shout or cry or die
instead I had to live a lie
and believe her when she said
I love you when we were abed,

I felt such a fool
to be a cuckold
as of stories told of men of old
who took for themselves
young wives to screw
who longed for young men
they quite well knew.

But I am not an old man
I did not marry a bride to screw
I brought her home
"for I love yous."

* * *

Aijar na mam edaun
(The life that never ends)

What if we live again
and the pain of death
is but in vain
because we all meet again,

We see each other
not as we were
but as we could be
living again
happy comfortable lives
free
as we should be,

Free from the pain we caused each other,

So your Daddy your sister
your Momma your wife
they may live again
and have a new life,

The difference is
they don't need us anymore
they all have
what they are looking for,

God is letting us know
they are free from the world below.

* * *

Charity

We have lived two thousand years
and never seen such torrential tears
fall for one who once was loved
now departed up above,

Clearly she must have been loved
for your cries reach heaven above
and all the pain and hurt you feel
would touch even a heart of steel,

This woman would when someone cried
run to help and not deride
she was always so full of love
so like an angel from above,

Yet she cannot now comfort those
ones who had for her
the most worth
for she is now there dead
although some wish to take her stead,

Yet we must all go on and live
and learn like her to always give
the charitable penny
and never to hate any.

Nature Poems

Licence to thrill
A good poet is like
Nalubaale
and as Saharan raindrops,

Being small and ubiquitous
one keeps trying.
* * *

Memory
The wind that blew woo
reminded me of you,

The sky was this blue
the last time I saw you.
* * *

Who likes emphasis in the vast view?
O vast view
what beauty ever saw you
as she who loves your view,

Is it the lover of fields
in clover
who deserves love
from those above,

I have seen some of those
once enthralled by stories told
of your nature's lovely folds,

They visit you
recall the view
and sing a lovely song of you,

O vast view
what beauty saw you
as she who isn't true,

She who once saw the view
and sang and sang of love for you,

How could it be you did not see
and sing of all that love to me,

How could you not tell me how
I could have made her take the vow,

For she knows I love her so
but she says I ain't no ho!

She knows I want to take her hand
and be the one to make her grand
if only she would understand,

But she insists a thousand grand
would maybe make her understand
how much I wish to be her man,

O vast view
what beauty saw you
fairer than she
who takes money for a view?

* * *

The selfish and (therefore) lonely star!

How can a star
burning bright
refuse to shine its light
upon the one due to die
a lone satellite?

* * *

Wrong advice to women!

Burn brightly
but do not shine your light
upon your one true satellite.

* * *

The Lion King

I am the wind in the trees
and the moon at night
the watery stream
and the sun so bright
the stars in the sky
a precious wind,

And I am with you
forever.

* * *

Life's bends

Like a tired old song
it just goes on
and on
sweeping us all along,

As if without end
it takes us
round the bend
without the time to make amends,

We see our friends come
we see our friends go
at times they close the door
and we see them no more,

To the ends of time
with its gentle rhyme
it takes us,

We live we die
and into dust
it breaks us,

Through its vast views
and it's sad news
of tragedy flowing
from majesty
it takes us,

On and on and on
it takes us
till we wonder
why we're born
it takes us,

Moving all along
on roads made of stones
like the tips of an arrow
till on the straight and narrow
when we're broken

and harrowed
we bend and cry,

Please hallow me
please hallow
please hallow me!

Then it takes us again.

* * *

Ode to autumn
I remember yesterday
when I thought
you were to stay
wished that in my arms
you'd lay
and you'd never go away,

I feel how I loved you
and I wished you'd
love me too
I'd have done it all for you
walked the mountains glaciers too,

For the tenderest flower
whose eyes were loving power
most beautiful of things
I'd have given everything,

Alas you were not there
when I said
I love you dear
if only I had said
Oh my love don't go away,

Now I stand here all alone
in my head I feel this song
through its tears I must be strong
though it's for you I still long.

* * *

If only
Sometimes in life you've
got to be strong
you've just and only
got to hold on,

Your spirit cries
within for release
when you want to fly
like the flock of wild geese,

Your spirit soars
high like a swift
as if imbued with a magical gift,

But all you can do is wonder why
with your head upraised to the
clouded sky,

You want to run wild and free
but all you can do
is be still and just be,

Your blood is screaming
for freedom screaming
to run like the wind all day
and be gone,

But all you can do
is stand all alone
or have a chat
on the telephone,

And then you say
I'm fine today
if only this rain would go away.
* * *

Thou art more than a conqueror, therefore relent
She the spirit from your past
sends these words and hopes they'll last,

She is like birds up in the sky
and the smile in a twinkling eye,

When choirs sing
till you want to cry
you wish that you were soaring high,

When the winds sing
and make you sigh
know it's she for she is nigh,

She is the sun and moon and stars
and the wind that sings for hours
so do not cry for love that's gone
for you will see your friend anon,

Remember then
my loyal friend
her love for you will never end.
* * *

On the way to Uppsala
The South wind blows
chasing the sun across the sky
hurling wet clouds
until they cover the sun,

All the while she's screaming
Come back here you whore
how dare you shine
on those you hardly know
how dare you expose yourself
to your own in-laws
come back here you whore!

And that is why Scandinavia is cold
because the sun shines there too.

* * *

Make it last forever!
Let's build a world
where we can live
where we don't take
more than we give,

A world where we have harmony
guarding against parsimony,

A world where man and creature
live happy peaceful lives
and fascinating features
make our world still worthwhile,

Let's build our world sustainably
and let the world that we still see
continue to be free,

Let's live as one in this world of ours
all races mixing in a whirl
communing with each other
for hours and hours and hours,

Loving one another
caring for each other
letting woman be a woman
and a man be a man
in this world of ours
forever.

Existentialist Poems

...me
When I look back
at the boy I used to be
I smile,

(Why smile at who
I used to be?)

It's because it used to
hurt to be…

* * *

Roll on the future!
Roll on my friends
roll on
even when the day is done
through frontiers and furlongs
we'll find a better dawn,

The world we're searching for
will soon become our own
the toils the troubles
the tears the struggles
will go away
no more one day
roll on my friends roll on
until a better dawn,

Roll on my friends
roll on
even when the day is done

through frontiers and furlongs
for 'tis a better dawn.

* * *

Open a new chapter
Little brother
don't let the world
tell you how to live
use your head
you have got so much to give,

Shape it
to your wants and needs
and help
the flower grow from the seeds,

Learn the beauty of the world
and let your love
be all unfurled,

The cynical ones who cast you out
won't be the ones who help you out
help you to get on your feet
when they succeed
and you're effete.

There is a beauty
which belongs
only to the rare and strong
so show us what is underneath
and be a man turn a new leaf,

Walk into a better world
of beauty laid out and unfurled.

* * *

The exile's song
I have been here a long time
and have seen this land's not mine,

My heart has burned
like a funeral pyre
made up of dreams
and strong desires,

Missing you
my darling and
remembering when
we were kissing dear
darling,

How long must I stay
before I'm free to go away
how long will it be
before again I know thee,

I count the days
and miss your ways
and remember the places
I stayed,

If only
I had stayed.

* * *

...surrounded by love
It has been some years
since we came
from then I knew
it would be the same,

We missed our brothers
who sang at the dawn_
and holding our heads up
and feeling no scorn,

People teased insulted abused
and then they said
Oh look he's amused,

Sometimes they were brothers
and sisters
though you'd have wondered if they were critters,

I have been denied love as a man
by those who thought they were cohorts and penned
for me misery
in a foreign land
so they could take Ariel's grand,

The grass is different
the trees are different
the sky the stars
are clearly not ours,

So I'll wait and wish
to see home's parish
be found again
then end this pain
and forever more
I'll live again,

And let it be once more spoken
I'm surrounded by love in the open.

* * *

Go white horses!

We're inside now
safe at last
we've made it at last
we're in first class,

The engines are roaring
preparing to blast
my concerns
and our fears away
as we leave this place
going today,

The engines are crying
a beautiful song
of freedom from loveless labour
so long,

The engines crescendo
tonnes of thrust
speed picks up
engines gust jet power
we go full blast,

Flight...

We are elated
gaining speed
could we be fated,

I looked into her eyes
and suppressed freedom cries
empathy for my pain
pulled me in love again.

* * *

My own man

I'm glad that I will live forever
because I know that I am a man
I want to climb the highest mountain
simply because I know that I can,

I want to walk across the desert
because it accords with my well laid plans
I want to build a business empire
and watch it thrive and grow and expand,

I want my business to grow and grow
and grow so I can be a titan
I want to be rich richer and richer
in all the ways that I possibly can,

All this is simply to say
I am my own man.

* * *

Proud of this form

Pride is the colour
of loneliness
which is the skeleton of pride,

It is not
a pretty colour
rather
it's an ugly pallor,

It forces us
to go on
even when we are weary
to the bone.

* * *

The Blues

It is these same blues
which remind me of those things
we used to do...

* * *

The Prince of Peace

Jesus is here
so do not fear
for he's the brilliance clear
his light burns the fear,

Jesus loves human love
we can have it too
if our hearts are true,

So do not fear
for Christ is here
with eyes of fire
cleansing all desire,

Let's worship him
with every part
and soon we may
have lion-hearts,

With Jesus
we'll move mountains
justice flow like fountains
the cynical sing love songs
for with him all can be strong,

In Jesus and prayer
we'll learn to share

our life and cares
with those who're dear,

Let's worship him
with all our hearts
and soon we may
be lion-hearts.

* * *

And on his law they meditate day and night
God loves the pure in heart
for they shall see their God
who fellowship with those you trust
and dwell within your word,

Bless all the pure in heart
whose fellowship depart
demons and knaves
that love you not
but worship the dark arts,

Bless them the pure in heart
to them your love impart
anoint those with your Spirit Lord
who daily trust your word,

Please make me pure in heart
I love you so my King
I worship cherish praise you
more than any other thing,

Dear Lord I pray allow
fulfilment of this vow
that I shall deserve to be
one of those who keep your vows,

Dear Lord my plea fulfil
the purpose of your will
and make me one of those who sups
with thee and tastes thy cups.

* * *

Rest in peace

Pray she enters dominion
where the darkness has not won
for the kindness she has shown
has inspired me to make song,

May my admiration flow
even though she's left us now
for I know one day somehow
we'll all meet at the rainbow,

For she is now beyond the stars
beyond these worlds of ours
and I have to be strong,

In a place where love is king
and we're bidden to come in
as family friends and kin,

And because of love forlorn
my heart in half is torn
and I sing my empty songs,

Some will miss her evermore
more than some of us may know
and I pray we'll meet anon,

For despite my different race
I came to accept my place
and even saw her State of Grace.

* * *

The eclectic dream

I dreamed
an electric dream...

At first,
I was struggling in a stream,...
against my own fantastic dream,

And then I heard a *lovely* song
which made my proud heart
yearn and long
for new horizons
and new zones,

In this song
I sang of Solara,
beauty... so fine and pure
she inspired awe
and made me gasp,

I was carried along by the feeling
of love and peace
electric eclectic harmony
brotherhood and manhood
and then my dream was gone.

* * *

She looked at me

And that look
will stay with me
for a period of eternity.

* * *

When the knight fell

And the music just sang on
as the devil took his soul,

Remorselessly it played
as his spirit fought and failed,

Beautiful soft gentle was the tune
yet evil bitter and vile was the doom,

How he fought how he flailed
knowing he would not prevail
for the ruler was too strong
and the music just sang on,

He was taken to a high place
by the ruler,

Wealth fame and the opulence of evil
he was shown
lust sex and power unknown
then when he was hungry
tempted by murder
manifest of the ruler's ardour,

Worship me, he said
for I'm ruler of the dead
yet that was not quite true
but the novice never knew,

I have killed your princess dear
with a word she reappears
worship me rule this galaxy
be a power further than anyone can see,

Bring her back
make her worship you
like a lord and husband
that she never knew,

But the novice could not see
that as he cried and bowed his knee
he would never again be free
till he did the same freely
to the Lord of all and thee,

And as he cried and bowed his knee
his princess still could see
that he prayed solely for her,

But the ruler meant to kill her
as soon as he could capture
the novice's mind
and be galactic wind,

And the ruler was too strong
yet the music just sang on,

The power of angels was given to him
he flew he foreknew he had every whim
he and the ruler then were like one
both trying to be the one true One,

Yet deep in his own fathoming he knew
he would never rule the galaxy
he flew and the ruler also knew,

He wanted to make everyone adore
the dark powers he got from below
to make up for the powers he could not afford
the power of the one true One,

Who is Lord,

But the novice fought and flailed
knowing he would not prevail
for the ruler was too strong
and the music just sang on,

And the music just sang on
as the devil took his soul,

Remorselessly it played
as his spirit fought
and failed...

Beautiful soft gentle was the tune
yet evil bitter and vile was the doom,

And he humbly bowed his knee
to the king
of that Galaxy,

But his heart
he kept it free.
* * *

Rage against the dying of the light

The eternal night...
you rest and yet you fight
until the murdered Saints sum right,

In the dark you have
your slumber
but be aware lest
you go under,

Your children and your wife
constantly miss your life
you hear them always calling
as you are slowly falling,

But journey on
for you are gone
and to the world
you don't belong,

So take your flight
with all your might
and enter rest eternally,

Heaven beckons you
so be a Christian too,

For don't you know
what the night can do?
* * *

Love always protects
The spirit of God
which dwells with his word
imparts to our hearts
love forgiveness all,

Hallelujah give thanks
to the Lord for His love

He blesses us all
and sends down His dove,

I love the Lord
the Holy One
He is the one
who made the sun,

He gives us light
so that we might
live in the light
not darkness fright,

Hallelujah give thanks
to the Lord for His love
He blesses us all
and sends down His dove,

He is the Lord
whose mighty word
demon's dark world
quickly erodes,

He saved us all
like lighting coal
the dark He lit
inside my soul,

Hallelujah give thanks
to the Lord for His love
He blesses us all
and sends down His dove,

Releasing our songs
in spring full of love

by sea horizons
beneath floating doves,

The sunshine trees
and birds and mist
the summer breeze
who can resist?

So praise the Lord
for all His love
He blesses all
with His Spirit's love,

Protect this world
it has great worth
if only for your lonely mirth,

Protect this world for future people
and give something
that is from us all.

* * *

A song of the dawn
Thank you God for loving us
thank you for forgiving us,

I begged you for a girlfriend
my friends said we would burn in hell
but you took everybody's curse
and instead saved us with a verse,

Thank you God for loving us
thank you for forgiving us,

I saw a lovely maiden
and wished to partner her for gain
and you said if I loved her
I should go up and ask her,

I know one day I'll marry
and you'll no longer carry
the burden of my loneliness
but instead fill my house with guests,

Thank you God for loving me
thank you for forgiving me,

You saved me from the evil arm
and to me restored happy calm,

You rescued me from fiery hell
because of something passionelle
and put me under orange trees
where leaves and branches shaded me,

Thank you God for loving me
thank you for forgiving me,

Your love always upholds me
although I put you on the tree
screaming for your blood
would that I understood,

Thank you God for loving me
thank you for forgiving me,

And despite sin you've saved me
though sin had taken hold of me
my heart was filled with hell
burning in a fiery hell,

Those evil passions Lord you fought
and fires of hell you made as nought,

Thank you God for loving me
thank you for forgiving me,

I was in the darkness
suffering from evil
but you lit the way
and put us on the level,

Thank you God for loving us
thank you for forgiving me,

In the darkest of the nights
our hearts had taken quite some fright
for we had to stand there and fight
against the hider of the light,

We were full of quivers
and really lily-livered
but peace came like a river
as we fought the deceiver,

Thank you God for loving us
thank you for protecting us,

Thank you for defending us
and reigning inside my heart,

Thank you God for loving us
thank you for protecting us,

Thank you for defending us
and for reigning in our hearts

Your life you gave upon the tree
just so we could all live freely,

Thank you Lord for loving us
thank you for forgiving us.

Love Poems

Even after death
I think I could love you
though the earth may be gone
and the sun is blue.

* * *

The end of eternity
As long as we love you and me
at the dawning of eternity.

* * *

To the real oasis?
You bring the rain
in searing heat
relief from pain,

I needed to eat
but 'twas no rain
but you brought it again,

Who'd have thought
I prayed not in vain
after praying for you
you brought the rain.

* * *

The dawning of eternity
To the ones who left here
how I wish you were still here
for I really miss your vibes

and your lovely
happy eyes,

Those teases and your smiles
oh I remember wiles
your love your earthy flair
and the friendship
we have shared,

I remember a time
when love's mountain we all climbed
and we saw each other's eyes
and began the blessed times.

* * *

Solara

Can a star
burning bright
refuse to shine its light
upon the one
due to die
as a satellite?

* * *

Beauty strikes!

In the dark I was inspired
her beauty shone
like she was afire,

She switched the light
exposed my fear
when she saw me hiding there,

A quiet rebuke
dispelled my fear

all was gone
for love and the fear.

* * *

Of a girl I loved to dream

Love burned a whole new course
when she stared straight to my soul,

She looked at me as if from a desert
whence vultures' withers
had steered poor trekkers
to lose their way to find the streams
in which were hidden all their dreams,

I do not know why she stared at me so
but she made me feel that we had to know,

She is still seeking the stream
yet I live as if I dream
merging with a pretty virgin
is what I wish wasn't a dream.

* * *

A young man dreams of courage

I saw a girl
she was playing so free
I wanted to show her
the places that we two could be,

Many places had I
but none of them was my own
for without that girl in my home
I felt so alone,

I should have told her...

Girl join me in my garden
love shouldn't grow old and burden
us with the guilt of playing a game
with prizes we can't claim,

So join me in my garden
and take away this burden
of loneliness and empty stress
without you in my arms.

* * *

Pride

Pride is the colour of loneliness
and loneliness is the skeleton of pride,

It leads to the abyss
that Dark Hole where none will miss
your true colours burning brightly
where no one ever sees thee,

We may love someone so true
yet we can never ever show
what we feel so deep inside
for our love may then deride,

Thus our sensitive ego
may rail and turn to evil
for in that moment of our love
as we go up on beauty's doves
bravely fearing nary
we find that she loves many,

So seek to give your heart away
and pray for love to save the day

then give away a penny
and love may help you marry.

* * *

Keep your best strength

Don't you know what the night can do
it often breaks even men more true,

Men hunger and they lust
for she who is not just
they think she is quite perfect
though their kids she won't protect,

Do not chase her my friend
for she will surely be your end
and you will end up lost
and broken for your costs,

The one you ought to want
is she without much cant
the one who'll give you smiles
that dazzle a long while,

When looking at her face
you'll wonder at such grace
she'll make you feel quite warm
through e'en the fiercest storm,

She can say I love you
yet never part her lips
and conjure in your mind
great somersaults and flips,

When you remember what she said
you'll want to take her to your bed,

Because she is your wife.

* * *

Diamonds love Racquel
Diamonds are forever
they last more than love's tethers,

We loved each other
I prayed it'd last forever
it's been a long time
since we were together,

I look at her picture,

We flew into each other's arms
and passion united thrilled and charmed
then we flew apart
each one for a new start,

We parted moving swifter apart
than any car could drive,

So when no one is in my life
I pray and try to live my life
without the love I got from her,

Memories of our love...
how she'd swoon and thrill with laughter,

I loved her,

I'm sitting in my garden
telling my love once again
why it can't be forever,

I look at her picture
does she live forever
then my heart remembers,

She left for life in Spain
and I may never hold her
nor ever love again
the way I loved in vain.

* * *

Ode to someone who used to be special

I will never hold you so
or look into those eyes of yours
and make you understand
my love unending like desert sands,

I long to hold you in my arms
and show you beauty scenes so calm
never seen so shining clear
as in those eyes so true and dear,

In that gaze we can do
anything you want us to
your Romeo I can be
as in romantic tragedy,

Those eyes of yours seem to know
what mine have seen and done before
they say the beauty mine have seen
is what at night they often dream,

But we have never touched alone
or slept together
felt so warm
the ecstasy of breaking free
into a world of eternity,

This romance is a tragedy.

* * *

Hope!

Right now I am feeling hurt
and alone
I feel as if I have not
a home
because she's left me
and she has gone,

Who knows how much
she meant to me
how much it was
I loved truly,

But she is not the only one
there are plenty more yet to come,

She's not the only
fish in the sea
there are plenty more
who may move me,

Love is how I felt for her
maybe she felt for me
but it also is the fact of
me respecting me,

Love is knowing how I
felt for her
will never ever die
but love must oft be tempered
by seeing reality,

I'll try to see that love is not
what puts food on my plate
clothes me upon my back
and maintains my estate,

But new love may take me away
from where old love refused to stay
and wash away the memory
of the friend that could not be.

* * *

Journey's song

I have heard a lovely song
and have felt its call so strong,

I have felt with heart afire
delighted by sounds of up higher,

And this song has carried me
up above the tops of trees,

Higher and faster and lighter it went
riding on singing with no relent
to the starlight on and on
and on to whole new worlds unknown,

Clarity and light came shining through
singing of a thousand views
telling me I should not fight
the one eternal guiding light,

The light is pure and without shade
it falls on all
virgin or jade
the radiance is here and glows
a fire burns a spark soars
from the spark comes a new fire
till soon the world is all afire,

This fire is love warm and soft
chasing the edges of winter off
till soon the winter turns to spring
and then the earth begins to sing,

This melody I heard in song
which came and carried me along
upon a journey far and long
began the everlasting song.

* * *

Ode to a foreigner

When we float above the clouds
and I see for me you're proud
then I'll know like stars above
that you have sincere love,

When you smile at me again
demonstrate I'm not in vain
then we'll break apart these chains
and the slavery will end,

When I see a butterfly
and no longer want to cry
then together we will fly
on a love none can deny,

When I hear you call my name
and you show you don't feel shame
then I'll know true love I've gained
and I will not feel ashamed,

When I look into your eyes
and it's clear I'll be in time
then we'll know true love we've found
even till we're underground,

When we fly above the clouds
and we speak without a word
then we'll know like turtle doves
that we are deep in love.

* * *

My gentle rhyme
Come my love
fly with me
across the winds of time
where we will go tripping
and skipping across time,

As young lovers we will fly
looking down below
at those who try
to make their lives better
without love,

And we will weep,

Let us see what we will see
as we walk on the clouds
on the air on the stars
and fascinate the crowds below
gazing up thinking,

They're some kind of portent or apparition
and we are,

Come with me
as we fly through space
and past these stars of ours,

And join with other people
who'll become friends at ours

Together we can be forever
as we'll stride hand in hand
into a new and bounteous place
a lovely holy land,

And the beauty is
we can live and love,

In a place where love's no sin
and we're all bidden to come in
and we will live
and live and live life
in worlds without end,

And may I bring you
my gentle rhyme?

* * *

Canadian blues of a Ugandan kid

I can hear eternity calling me
with a thousand voices
voices of the past and future
ancestors gone before me,

I can hear it calling me
pulling me
closer and closer,

Singing its enchanting
siren song siren song
singing its enchanting song
enchanting siren song,

I can see her calling me
begging me
please be strong
please be strong,

I can hear her crying
across the ocean
across the vast seas
I am calling out her name
I am calling her name,

My love has lasted an eternity
that is how far she is from me
yesterday has said so long
here I stand all alone,

Oh trans-Atlantic love
your love's in
an eternity of distance...

* * *

Canadian blues by a Ugandan man

He's got the Canadian blues again
that's when the feelings
of love for her run
then he can't live anywhere but
under Canada's sun,

Nor can love anyone
but a Canadian named
_____,

No twilight can be so beautiful
as that he'd see with her

and no dawn can ever be so full of love
as that they'd share forever
in love ,

To feel the red and gentle sun
ripening the fruits anon
blue skies, yews, rolling views
would make him feel at home,

Finding a love like the one he had
would make him want to stay
and teach World Bank economics
just so they could play,

Canadian blues...
I miss you,

At dawn the trees are green
with the light gentle red yellow sun
shining up through the trees
as he looks ahead at them,

Birds' songs chit chittering
bright sounds as in a dream
to wake up is a new dream,

At sunset it's red white and blue
the sky gets dark
a lovely view,

Standing by the sea
watching it rolling back
he dreams of going home to her
it makes his eyes react,

Instead of far shores and heydays
he wants his former lady,

Oh Canadian blues
I miss you.

* * *

Ode to an angel
Those were our days
I wish they were always
but soon new days will be
and you'll remember me,

Remember the first kiss
oh there were some before
but that was the best one
the one I miss much more,

It was in the dark
after playing in the park
then the lights were bright
as we made it all right,

Those were our days
and soon new days will come
but please always remember girl
to me you were the one.

* * *

To the successful Messiah - what a way to win!
Lord, do not deny the pain
you felt when you died
I know you suffered
which is why I cried,

If only I could make all of the others see
the pain you bore
your love given freely,

The thousands who bayed for your blood
I wish they could all have understood
how sad you were
sad at those who laughed aloud
at your disciples and drew lots
because they comprehended naught,

We knew we sinned
yet we still made an evil din
Crucify him
yet we needed forgiving,

We chose instead to destroy
what we could not alloy
holy love mercy
the incarnate Deity,

But now you are alive
the Lord who heard my cry
opened his arms and died
gave everlasting life
that no-one can deny,

Saved everlasting life
that no-one can deny.

* * *

Show a little tenderness
I love to look at her pretty face
it gives me joy
when she smiles at me,

After having worked hard
and losing at cards
I remember a film
where the heroine dies
and yet nobody cries
the message seems too bad,

Then she comes to me
and all the stress
is washed away
leaving me feeling new
ready for a new day,

I can look in her eyes
and see us
walking with love
in a bounteous orchard
or bucolic vineyard
with new-born butterflies
fluttering floating around.

* * *

Dreams may come true
Waking up beside her each morning
when we're at home
would help my world keep turning
towards the dawn,

Despite the Fall I'd be with her
love enduring despite winter,

We'd awake to snow over everything
and childish screams of snow fighting,

We'd float in love over paradise
our love revealed with no disguise,

Romance through valleys green
through orchards vineyards streams,

Then when inside we'd kiss
forgetting those we miss
enjoying quiet bliss
of love and inner peace,

It would mean that I could show
the feelings within me
and keep winning her heart
yet let it still be free,

It'd mean we'd marry
and that she'd carry our child
and we'd stay happy.
* * *

**A scene we shared beneath the stars
in days gone by**
I'm just drinking this drink
and stinking this stink
because no matter what I think
it's the only way I know to live,

I've had my share of hotel rooms
and seen my fill of bluebell blooms
I've lived through countless scores of glooms
and seen my fill of eclipsed moons,

All that time I've spent alone,
you'd think: "This man never had a home."
and even though some nights I roam

the streets as if I have no home
I can recall a friendly scene
I shared with friends
who too could dream,

A scene we shared beneath the stars
we talked and talked for hours and hours
of this and that and each man's scars
and watched and wished upon the stars
silently in the small hours,

Then drink and sleep as if at home
and we'd be long gone after gloam,

Such scenes we'd have every week
and then back home be mild and meek
we'd suffer and struggle a week
then meet our friends again and speak
and walk down to the pub in rain
and drink and talk and laugh again.

Tomorrow to the pub we'd go
for a pub breakfast and hello.

* * *

Lord

Lord of the earth and sky
hear my humble cry,

Though through your Son
you died
when you were crucified,

You are alive
and here today

the one who died
not gone away,

And so I pray
you'll hear me pray
"Abide Lord in my heart always."

* * *

Now the trek is over

Even though it breaks your hearts
remember friends
times not apart,

The love we shared
the joys so rare
even though
we are not there,

Though it is all in the past
we know in our minds it lasts,

So till the next time again
if here on earth or up in heaven
bye my friends live long and gain,

And remember us
time and again,

For I will remember you
and those things we used to do
and our friendships will go on
even when our lives have gone,

So remember us my friends
we'll still be friends even when life ends

though we're far apart
we're in each other's hearts.

* * *

Brothers and sisters...
Brothers cousins friends
we have all grown up
all reached the end
of the growing days,

We have all changed
in small ways
but still we remain the same
the friendship proved
not in vain,

Some of us are Asian
some of us American
some of us European
some of us love everyone,

Though we have to fight
at the weekend
we make things right,

Though our strivings don't cease
we strive to foster peace
create love and harmony
and seek to end parsimony,

We live in our homes
and make up love songs
respect each other's lives
and share so we can live,

We wonder apart
but in the end
we make a new start
for we are friends.

* * *

Time and tide wait for no-one
Don't leave it too late
to repent of the past
and the unsaved life
that you can't recast,

Don't leave it too late
to communicate
with the one you know
gave life to our world,

You know it's true
when you stand on the shore
surveying the sea
rolling out from the shore
and dream,

Of far skies to watch the dawn view
before you know
you've lived your life through
and retire to the other side of sands
that wait for no man and tide,

You've heard it in the echoes of your mind
and in the murmurs of the wind,

You know it's true so pray,
In case you doubt
Satan couldn't have made you,

You have a certain beauty or purity in you
which is too strong
inside your eyes
the morning star shines on,
It is your yearning for some great prize
perhaps to be loved above all others
and to love above all others
to see the extent of one's own love
and beauty revealed to all,

That is what marks you out as one
who is seeking God,

That desire is of God
a yearning of the human spirit
to be embraced by its maker,

To fulfil that desire seek God's face
in anger's place
his mercy and grace
let hurt erase
and forgive for you have a life to live.

* * *

www.ingramcontent.com/pod-product-compliance
Lightning Source LLC
Chambersburg PA
CBHW010642240426
43663CB00050B/2911